DISCOVERING CANADA

NewFrance

ROBERT LIVESEY & A.G. SMITH

Fitzhenry & Whiteside

First published in 1990 by
Stoddart Publishing Co. Limited

Published in Canada
by Fitzhenry & Whiteside,
195 Allstate Parkway,
Markham, Ontario L3R 4T8

www.fitzhenry.ca

Published in the United States
by Fitzhenry & Whiteside,
311 Washington Street,
Brighton, Massachusetts 02135

godwit@fitzhenry.ca

10 09 08 4 5 6

Canadian Cataloguing in Publication Data

Livesey, Robert, 1940 –
New France

(Discovering Canada)
Includes index.
ISBN 978-0-7737-5341-9

1. Canada – History – To 1763 (New France) – Juvenile literature.   2. Canada – Discovery and exploration – French – Juvenile literature. 3. Canada – Social conditions – To 1763 – Juvenile literature. I. Smith, A. G. (Albert Gray), 1945–   II. Title.   III. Series: Livesey, Robert, 1940–   Discovering Canada.

FC305.L58 1990   j971.01   C90-093506-5   F1030.L58 1990

*Fitzhenry & Whiteside acknowledges with thanks the Canada Council
for the Arts, the Government of Canada through its Book Publishing
Industry Development Program, and the Ontario Arts Council for
their support in our publishing program.*

Printed and bound in Canada

To Betty and Edna, with love

Special thanks to Sister Jean Livesey, Sister Teresa Burgess, Beverley Sotolov-Anderson, Darlene Money, the librarians at the Oakville Public Library, the Sheridan College Library and the University of Windsor Library for their help in producing this book.

Table of Contents

Introduction

The brave men and women from Europe who were the first permanent settlers in Canada were daring heroes and heroines, and their stories tell of great achievements, greedy villains, fateful tragedies and adventurous conquests.

The first book in this series, *The Vikings*, reported the failure of the first European settlements in Canada in 1,000 A.D. After Columbus rediscovered the New World in 1492, gold and other riches from Central and South America were exported to Spain. Immediately other countries were eager to explore America.

In 1497 King Henry VIII financed an expedition by Venetian sea captain Giovanni Caboto (John Cabot) to America to make an English claim. Cabot landed in Newfoundland, which was rich in fish rather than gold. English fishing ports with stores and drying flakes soon sprang up along the Newfoundland coast. Winter crews lived in "fishing rooms," and facilities to repair or supply ships became available at St. John's.

By 1534 King François I, determined to establish a French outpost, had hired an adventurous sea captain, Jacques Cartier, who explored the coast of Newfoundland, Prince Edward Island and the Gaspé Peninsula. Cartier reported that the Indians were eager to trade furs:

*They bartered all they had to such an extent that all went back naked —
and they made signs to us that they would return on the morrow with
more furs.*

He returned in 1535 and sailed up the St. Lawrence River to the
Iroquois village of Stadacona (present-day Quebec City). The chief,
Donnacona, welcomed the visitors. Cartier then proceeded up the
river to another Indian village, Hochelaga, (present-day Montreal),
where he and his men were again greeted:

*Great numbers of the inhabitants came out to meet us and give us a
hearty welcome...the girls and women of the village crowded about us,
rubbing our faces...weeping for joy at the sight of us.*

Cartier returned to Stadacona, where he spent a cold winter at the
harbour (November 1535–April 1536). All his 110 men, except for
10, became sick with scurvy, and 25 died.

*Their legs became swollen and inflamed, with sinews shrunken and black
like charcoal...then the disease would rise to the hips, shoulders, arms and
neck...all had their mouths so infected that gums rotted down to the roots
of the teeth, nearly all of which fell out.*

In 1541 the king appointed Roberval governor and instructed
him to establish a French colony with 10 ships, 400 sailors, 300 soldiers, skilled tradesmen and a few women. Jacques Cartier was
made navigator of the expedition. But Roberval's ships were
delayed, and Cartier, who was impatient, left without him.

When Cartier discovered gold and diamonds, he loaded his ships
with the treasure and headed home. On the way back, he met
Governor Roberval, who ordered Cartier to stay with him to estab-

lish a colony at Cap Rouge, but that night Cartier slipped away, anxious to return to France with his rich cargo.

Roberval's colony survived only one year. Cartier's treasure turned out to be "fool's gold" and the diamonds were common quartz. In France an expression became popular to describe anything that was worthless — *un diamant de Canada*.

Children as Gifts

It was the Indian custom to seal a friendship by giving away their children. Chief Donnacona gave Cartier three children: a ten-year-old girl and two younger boys. As Cartier proceeded up the river to Richelieu Rapids, another chief gave him a child.

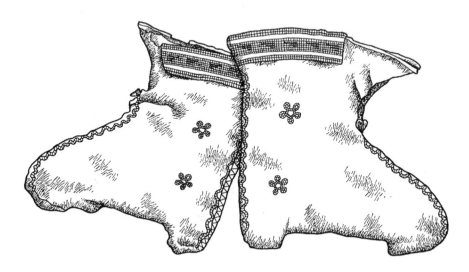

Indian moccasins taken back to France by Cartier.

How Canada Got Its Name

When Cartier encountered the Iroquois chief Donnacona in the village of Stadacona, he called him *"le seigneur de Canada,"* thinking that "Canada" was the name of the country. However, Canada in the Indian language meant "village."

Magical Cure

When Cartier's crew developed scurvy, the Indians had a cure. Evergreen twigs were boiled in water. The patients then drank the water and rubbed the residue on their sores. Even men who had suffered from scurvy for eight years were cured immediately. The tree was probably a white cedar; the magic was vitamin C.

Kidnapped Chief

When he was getting ready to return to France in 1536, Cartier invited Chief Donnacona to visit him. Suddenly he kidnapped the chief and four other braves. The next day the tribe collected their total wealth, 24 strings of wampum, and tried to buy back their leader. Cartier refused, saying he would return the next year with his captives after he had shown them to the French king. The Indians all died in France, probably of smallpox. When Cartier returned five years later, he lied, saying that they were living "as great lords" in France. But the Iroquois did not believe him; they became enemies of the French.

Marooned Lovers

In 1541 when Governor Roberval set out to create a colony at Cap Rouge, his young niece, Marguerite de la Roche, was with him. She fell in love with a young man on the ship, but her uncle ordered them to stay apart. With the help of Marguerite's old servant, Damienne, the two young people continued to meet. When the furious uncle discovered the truth, he marooned the three of them on the uninhabited island of Fugo with only guns and ammunition.

That winter their food ran out and the young man died, but a baby was born to Marguerite. She became a good hunter and even shot a polar bear. But her baby died, too, as well as her loyal servant. She buried them beside her lover and managed to survive a second freezing Canadian winter alone. After two years and five months, she was finally rescued by a French fishing vessel.

1

Father of New France

Samuel de Champlain

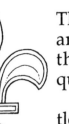

There are all kinds of people in the world. Some are wise and plan for the future; others live for the moment, rarely thinking about the consequences of their actions.

In 1603 Samuel de Champlain arrived at the settlement of Tadoussac (where the Saguenay River enters the St. Lawrence). In the first year only 5 of 16 colonists had survived, but Champlain was a man with a vision. He was devoted to colonizing New France, converting the native peoples to Christianity, developing a rich fur trade and charting the unexplored wilderness.

The next year, 1604, Champlain joined the de Monts expedition to create a new colony on an island in the Ste-Croix River, but 35 of 79 men died of cold or disease, and 20 were near death. The following year, 1605, the survivors moved to Port Royal, where Champlain and about 40 companions remained for another winter.

The history of New France truly began when Champlain and de Monts founded a fur trading settlement in 1608 at what is today Quebec City. Champlain built his famous *habitation* of wooden buildings protected by a palisade of logs, then returned to France, leaving 22 men to face a deadly winter. Only 8 survived, one of them a 15-year-old boy named Etienne Brûlé.

Brûlé was a healthy, adventurous youth whose personality was the opposite of Champlain's. Champlain was to earn the title "Father of New France"; Brûlé was more like the "Juvenile Delinquent of New France."

After two boring, cold winters confined to the tiny settlement, Brûlé begged Champlain to allow him to live with the Indians. Champlain agreed, exchanged Brûlé for a Huron brave of the same age and returned to Paris to show off his "human prize." Brûlé became the first *coureur de bois* (runner of the woods), learned to speak several Indian languages and adopted the free but rough life of the native people.

Brûlé kept no records of his exploits. The only descriptions of his activities were written by the priests, who objected to his lifestyle and his unholy marriages to Indian women. Champlain wrote of Brûlé:

This man was recognized as being very vicious in character and much addicted to women.

Yet Brûlé was the first white man to travel up the Ottawa River, portage overland to Georgian Bay and visit all of the five Great Lakes. He followed Indian trails from present-day Toronto to Niagara Falls. When he returned with stories of his travels, no one believed him.

It was Champlain, using Brûlé as a guide and interpreter, who made the first charts of the Ottawa River and Georgian Bay. When Champlain agreed to help his Huron friends fight a rival tribe known as the Andastes, he relied on Brûlé to scout ahead with a party of 200 Hurons. Brûlé was to meet with Champlain and the main Huron war party at the Andaste village, but he failed to show up. Champlain was defeated and he returned to Quebec furious.

The final break between Champlain and Brûlé came in 1629 when England and France were at war. Brûlé was sent to Tadoussac to pilot a French vessel up the St. Lawrence River. Instead, when he encountered Sir David Kirke and the British fleet, Brûlé and the other *coureurs de bois* who were with him joined the English and piloted Kirke up the river, where he captured Quebec and took Champlain prisoner.

After the war Britain gave New France back to France, and in 1633, Champlain returned as governor. He died at Quebec in 1635.

Mysterious Death

One of the strangest events in the history of New France was the death of Etienne Brûlé in June 1633. For some unknown reason the Bear tribe, with whom he had lived for years, tortured and killed him. Then they scattered in guilt and fear of the ghost of Brûlé.

The Order of Good Cheer

During the winter of 1605, Poutrincourt, the *seigneur* of Port Royal, started a special club, *L'Ordre de Bon Temps* (The Order of Good Cheer), in which each member took his turn supplying a dinner for the others. It was served with great ceremony.

The ruler of the feast...having had everything prepared by the cook, marched in, napkin on shoulder, wand of office in hand, and around his neck the collar of the Order...after him all the members of the Order, carrying each a dish.

Governors of New France

Samuel de Champlain	1612-1629
	1633-1635
Charles Jacques de Huault de Montmagny	1636-1648
Louis de Coulonge d'Ailleboust	1648-1651
Jean de Lauzon	1651-1656
Pierre de Voyer, Vicomte d'Argenson	1658-1661
Pierre Dubois, Baron d'Avaugour	1661-1663
Augustin de Saffray Mézy	1663-1665
Daniel de Rémy, Sieur de Courcelle	1665-1672
Louis de Buade, Comte de Frontenac	1672-1682
Joseph-Antoine Lefèvre de La Barre	1682-1685
Jacques René de Brisay, Marquis de Denonville	1685-1689
Louis de Buade, Comte de Frontenac	1689-1698
Louis Hector de Callières	1699-1703
Philippe de Rigaud, Marquis de Vaudreuil	1703-1725
Charles, Marquis de Beauharnois	1726-1747
Roland Michel Barin, Comte de La Jonquière	1749-1752
Ange Duquesne, Marquis de Menneville	1752-1755
Pierre de Rigaud, Marquis de Vaudreuil-Cavagnal	1755-1760

Young Bride

It was the custom for girls to marry at an early age, not only in the Indian villages and early settlements but in the royal court of France. In the winter of 1610-1611, Champlain, 43, arranged to marry Helen Boulle, 12, daughter of the king's secretary.

Champlain and two men, wearing steel breastplates and helmets, carried arquebuses. The Hurons, decorated with war paint, led him into what is today Vermont and New York states, where they found an Iroquois village. A party of 200 Iroquois, who had not seen guns before, attacked the intruders.

I took aim with my arquebus and shot straight at one of the three chiefs, and with this shot two fell to the ground, and one of their companions was wounded, who died thereof a little later...seeing their chiefs dead, they lost courage and took to flight, abandoning the field and their fort, and fleeing into the depth of the forest.

First Gunshots

In July 1609 Champlain agreed to help his Huron friends fight their enemy, the Iroquois.

The Company of 100 Associates

In 1627 Cardinal Richelieu decided to organize the settlement of New France. He formed a new company with a ten-year monopoly on the fur trade. In return, the company had to finance the colony and agree to send 4,000 settlers within 15 years. To stop the disputes that had occurred between the Catholics and the non-Catholic Huguenots, he barred all Protestants from New France.

Canada's First Slave

When Kirke captured Quebec in 1629, he brought with him a black youth he had purchased in Madagascar. Although the native people of Canada sometimes made slaves of their enemies, this was the first slave imported to Canada. Kirke sold the boy to the town clerk, Louis Le Bailly. Over a period of 125 years there were more than 4,000 slaves in New France. About 1,200 were blacks from the West Indies. Most were very young and died on average at 17 or 18 years of age.

Well-fed Colonists

The colonists at Port Royal in 1604–1605 used brick ovens to bake stone-ground whole wheat bread. Their menu included seafoods such as mussels, crabmeat, sturgeon and lobster and they grew vegetables such as corn, squash, beans and cabbages. Tender moose meat and delicate beaver tail were also part of their diet.

Early Navigation (the Astrolabe)

Early sailors and explorers depended on the sun, the stars and the horizon to "guess" at their course and position. The astrolabe was an improvement over the sundial and could be used to calculate a ship's latitude. In 1624 sailors were also using the cross-staff, the quadrant, the sector and the globe to locate their positions. By the 1700s the sextant was invented, which finally turned navigation into a science.

· **SOMETHING TO DO** ·

Make an Astrolabe

What you need:
scissors
hobby knife
white glue
poster board
yellow crayon or marker
paper punch
a paper fastener
string

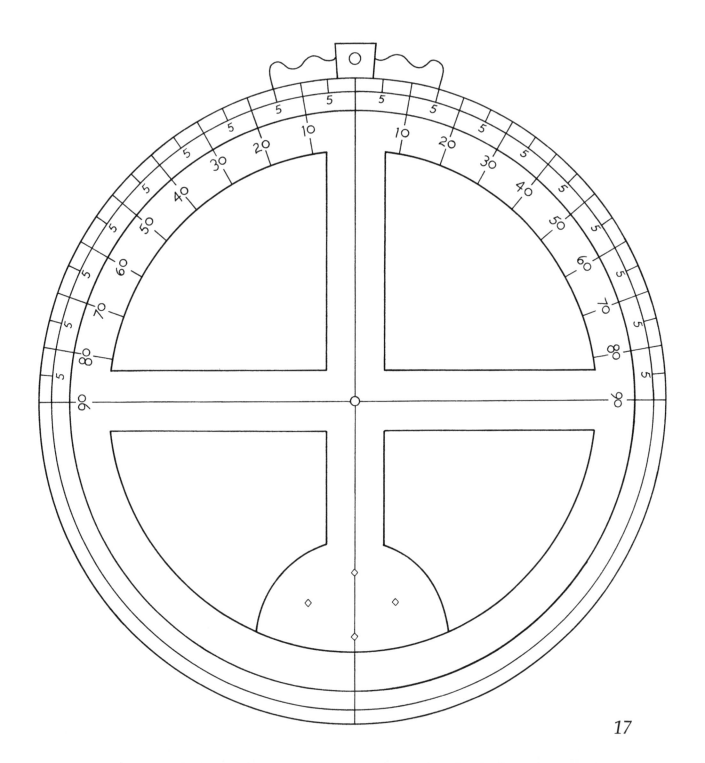

17

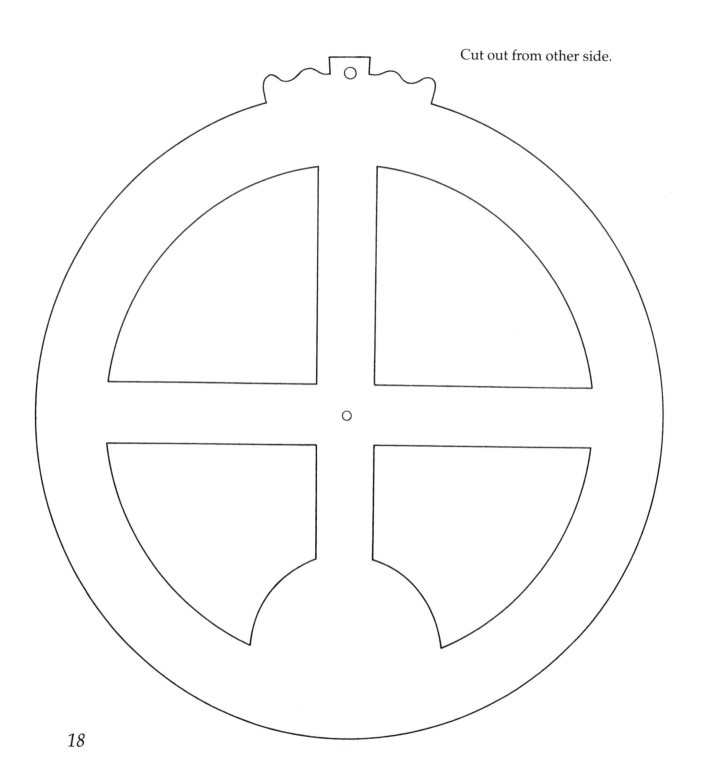

Cut out from other side.

18

What to do:

1. Glue the astrolabe disc and arm to poster board. Apply the glue in a very thin layer to prevent wrinkling and seepage.

2. Cut out the disc and arm.

3. Cut out the sights and glue each sight back to back (see Fig. 1). After the sights have dried, punch out the sight holes with a paper punch.

4. Colour the pieces yellow to resemble brass. (Do not colour the inside of the tabs on the sights or on the places marked to receive them on the arm.)

5. Glue the sights to the arm (see Fig. 2).

6. Attach the arm to the disc using a paper fastener.

7. Tie a loop of string about 40 cm long through the hole in the top of the disc.

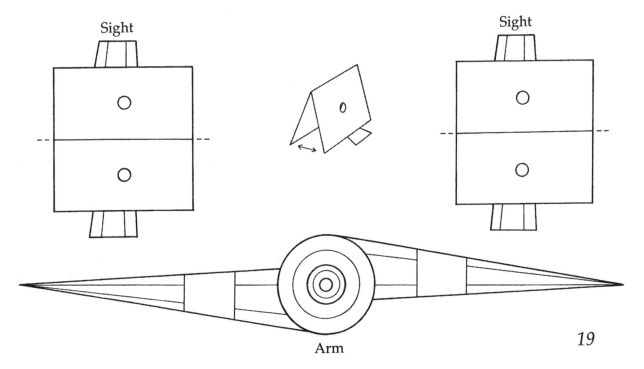

Sight

Sight

Arm

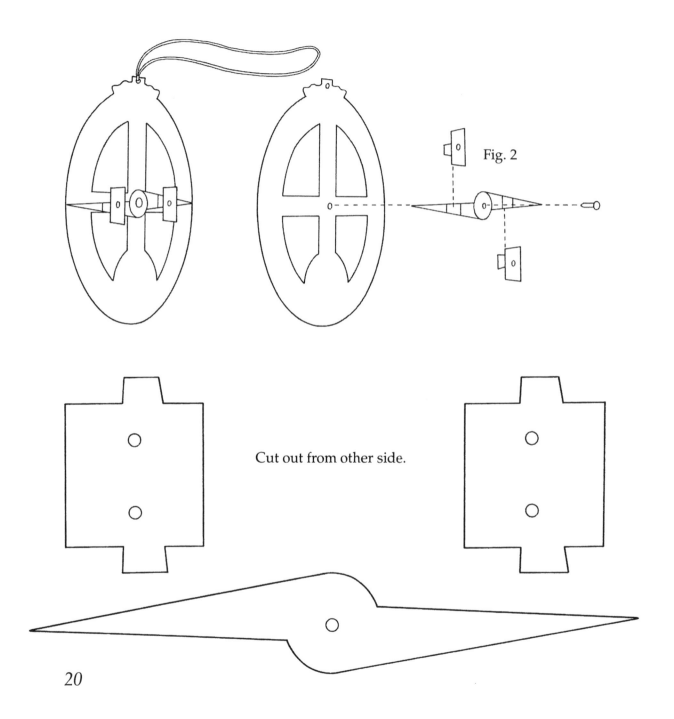

Fig. 2

Cut out from other side.

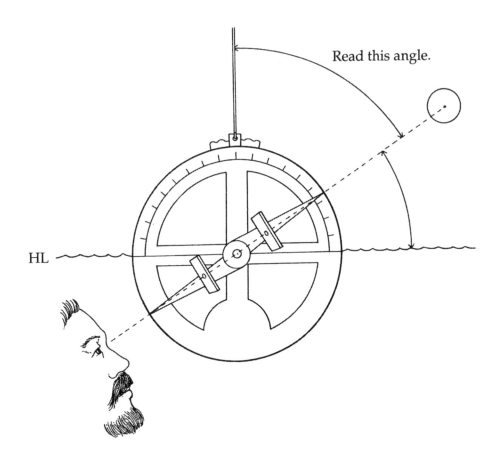

Read this angle.

HL

How the use your Astrolabe:

1. Suspend the astrolabe so that the centre line on the disc is level with the horizon line (HL).

2. Sight the object (a star or the sun) through the sight pieces. Now read the angle and sub-tract it from 90 degrees. If you use the North Star the angle will also be your approximate latitude.

CAUTION: If you sight the sun, do not stare at it for more than a moment.

2 *Battle for Acadia*

Marie La Tour

If you watch the news on TV or read the newspapers, you know that human beings are always arguing or fighting. People in New France were no different. When they were not battling the Indians or fighting with the British, the French were squabbling among themselves.

Charles La Tour, ten years old, arrived in New France with his father in 1610; by 1640 he had become the lieutenant-governor of Acadia. His bride, Marie, newly arrived from France, was a Huguenot, not a Catholic like Charles. She wrote home:

The summer is beautiful. My Charles says the sea moderates our winters, and we have all the wood in the world, spacious fire-places, and love to keep us warm.

Marie became not just Charles's wife, but his partner in business, politics and war. When Charles travelled in search of furs, Marie took command of the fort, even as she tended her newborn son.

But all was not peaceful in her new home at Fort La Tour (in present-day New Brunswick). Across the Bay of Fundy at Port Royal (in present-day Nova Scotia), she and Charles had a deadly rival, another lieutenant-governor of Acadia, Sieur de Charnisay. They had conflicting land grants, and the headquarters of each was in the middle of the territory claimed by the other.

Charnisay was related to Cardinal Richelieu, who was very powerful in France. A royal decree charged Charles with treason; a court order stated that La Tour, his fort and all its contents were to be seized. In those days, if a person had powerful enemies, he or she could be locked up without a trial in the infamous French prison called the Bastille.

In 1643 Charnisay blocked the harbour of Fort La Tour with six ships and a force of 500 men. After a month of siege, a ship, the *St. Clement*, arrived. It had been sent by the Protestants in France to aid the La Tours. On a foggy night, Marie and Charles slipped daringly past the blockade in a small boat and escaped in the *St. Clement* to Boston, where the English governor gave them men and ships. They returned and, during a swift-running sea battle, chased an angry Charnisay back to Port Royal.

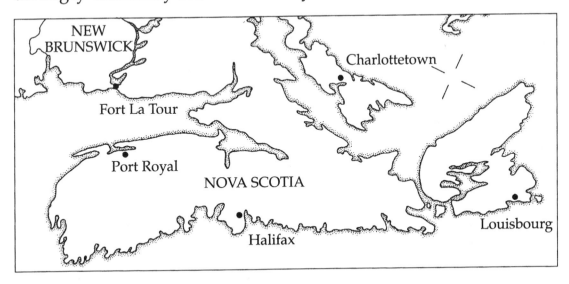

Map of Acadia

Marie sailed to France to seek more help from Protestant allies, but Charnisay's friends had a death penalty placed on her head. She escaped to England and sailed back to Acadia in the *Gillyflower*. Charnisay stopped, boarded and searched the English ship, but Marie, hiding in the hold, was not discovered. At Boston she obtained three ships and supplies, and returned defiantly in 1644.

The following February, when Charles was away collecting furs, two Catholic friars reported to Charnisay that Fort La Tour had a garrison of only 45 men. The attack came instantly, but during the bloody battle Marie beat back the invaders. A few weeks later, Charnisay returned with reinforcements and ordered the surrender of Fort La Tour. Marie put on her steel breastplate and helmet and hung out the red flag of combat.

Huge cannonballs smashed against the seaward walls of the wooden fortress as Charnisay landed his troops, who attacked in waves. Marie and her followers used pikes and halberds to prevent the enemy from scaling the walls. Outnumbered five to one, the defenders held out for four days. On Easter Sunday, as Marie and the others prayed in the chapel, a guard who was secretly in the pay of Charnisay let the attackers inside the fort. But as they poured over the unguarded walls, Marie charged from the church with her small band and forced them to retreat.

There was no hope of rescue; defeat was certain. When the deceitful Charnisay sent Marie an offer to surrender, she accepted on the condition that no one would be harmed. Charnisay agreed, but once he had control of the fort, he ordered all the garrison hanged. With a rope around her neck, Marie watched all her loyal followers go to their deaths. She was not executed immediately, but died mysteriously three weeks later while in Charnisay's custody.

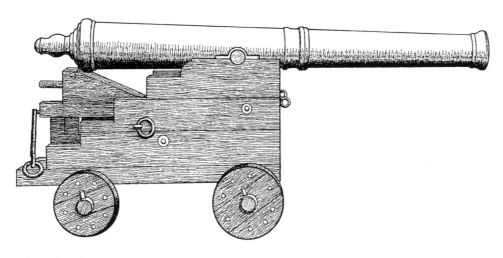

Death of Charnisay

A few years after Marie La Tour's death, Charnisay drowned in the river at Port Royal. An Indian whom Charnisay had beaten rescued Charnisay's servant but left the cruel master to die.

Strange Marriage

In 1653 Charles La Tour married Charnisay's widow, Jeanne. The marriage served as a peace treaty that established Charles as governor of all Acadia.

Capture of Port Royal

In 1710 an English force of 1,900 captured Port Royal from 258 defenders and claimed all Acadia. They renamed Port Royal "Annapolis Royal" and called the colony "Nova Scotia."

The rich gentlemen who purchased large tracts of land, much like private kingdoms or dukedoms, were called *seigneurs*. They did not work the land themselves but divided it into smaller lots and gave tenant farmers, called *habitants*, titles in return for a portion of their crops or a few days' work on the *seigneur*'s farm. The *habitant* was not a labourer but a land owner who could buy or sell his property.

The land grants all included access to the river for fishing and transportation. As *habitants* divided their land among their children, the farms became narrower strips along the river front.

The island of Montreal was originally a small *seigneurie*. Some large grants ran from the St. Lawrence River to the Atlantic coast. One grant included 280 km (180 mi.) of river frontage.

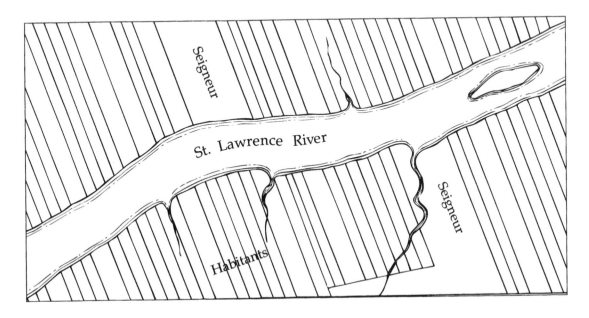

Fashions in New France

What to do:
1. Photocopy the people on pages 28-31.
2. Using the descriptions as a guide, colour the costumes. Use flesh tones for the faces and limbs.

Pierre's attire is fit for a governor. His steel-gray hat and bucket boots are trimmed with silver gray. The white-lace collar matches the white-lace frill on his silk stockings. His dark-blue cassack is decorated with silver buttons and braiding. His right arm is slung inside, with his protruding hand clutching a glove.

Marie is fashionably dressed as a young lady of New France. Her overskirt is magenta, contrasting with her bright-yellow underskirt, which is embroidered with red and gold stripes. Her white, double-frill cuffs accent the wide, fan-shaped collar, and she carries a stylish fan.

François, a merchant-adventurer, wears a dark-green cape with gold braiding and lining. His white collar and cuffs set off his burgundy dag-edged doublet and panes (ballooned breeches). In his hand he carries a broad-brim cavalier cap of black beaver. The off-white leggings are highlighted by the mustard ribbon garters and rosettes above his shoes.

Pierre

Marie

François

29

Natalie represents a typical servant girl, with her white bonnet and apron. Her linen blouse is a pale yellow with elbow-length sleeves and her woollen skirt is a plain brown. She carries a blue ceramic jug.

Little Doe, an Iroquois maiden, is wearing a copper ornament around her neck. Her fringed outfit, in natural tones of yellow and brown, is made entirely of soft deerskin. The colourful bead trim around her shoulders matches the same on her moccasins. She carries a cedar bow in her hand. (Before Caucasians arrived with beads, the Indians decorated their costumes with porcupine quills, dyed with wild berries.)

White Eagle is a proud Iroquois warrior with a Mohawk haircut. His face and chest are decorated with war paint as colourful as the feathers on the arrows in the quiver on his shoulder. His coal-black loincloth is hung from a red-and-white waistband and decorated with bright-coloured bead trim, as are his wampum belt, armband and moccasins. The deerskin leggings are tied at the knees with rawhide strips.

Natalie

30

Little Doe

White Eagle

3 *The Giant Black Robe*

Jean de Brébeuf

Throughout history people have had different religions and philosophies. Sometimes their beliefs are so strong that they are willing to die for them. Such people are called martyrs.

In New France religion was a strong force that controlled all aspects of life in the colony. The first black-robed Jesuits arrived in New France in 1525, eager to convert the native people to Christianity. One priest, Father Jean de Brébeuf, towered over the Hurons; he was 200 cm (6 ft. 8 in.) tall. He spent 23 years in Huronia and founded five missions.

As a young man Brébeuf travelled 1,290 km (780 mi.) by canoe to work with the Hurons at St. Ignace (present-day Midland, Ontario). He kept a diary and was one of the first to record the westward trail. It took six patient years before he gained his first adult convert to Christianity. Brébeuf learned the Huron language and composed a dictionary and grammar book for his people's use. When the white man's diseases killed thousands of native people, the priests were blamed, and in 1637–1638 Brébeuf watched the Hurons tear down his crosses and even stone and torture his fellow Jesuits. He endured it all and won back their respect with his religious zeal.

When fleeing Indians arrived at his village on March 16, 1644, warning that 1,000 Iroquois were close behind them, Brébeuf knew

33

what would happen to him if he remained. He had heard the tales of horror, torture and death the year before when the villages of St. Joseph and St. Michel were overrun. The Iroquois especially hated white missionaries, whom they considered cowards because they wore the "black skirts of women." Nevertheless Brébeuf's choice was clear: it was his land and they were his people; he would stay with 80 warriors to resist the attackers.

Brébeuf's small band of Hurons was defeated and he was captured. The Iroquois drove him with clubs and stones back to St. Ignace. There he was tied to a stake in the log church that he had constructed with his own hands. They stripped off his "woman's robes," beating and torturing his naked body. Brébeuf was determined not to cry out or show weakness because he knew the Indians respected boldness, courage and strength in suffering.

Wishing to break his spirit and faith, the Iroquois tortured him for four hours. The torments he endured are considered the most atrocious and hideous ever suffered by Christian martyrs. The only sound Brébeuf made was to pray for the Iroquois. He died, but with his death came victory. The Iroquois saluted an enemy undefeated by torture, the greatest compliment they could pay him. Legends of the unmatched courage of the giant black robe spread through Huron villages and the number of converts to Christianity grew.

Patron Saint of Canada

On June 29, 1930, three centuries after his death, Brébeuf was canonized by Pope Pius XI. On October 16, 1940, he was proclaimed patron saint of Canada. His feast day is September 26.

Bishops of New France	
François de Montmorency Laval	1674-1688
Jean Baptiste de La Croix Chevrière de Saint-Vallier	1688-1727
Louis François Duplessis de Mornay	1727-1733
Pierre Hermann Dosquet	1733-1739
François Louis Pourroy de Lauberivière	1739-1740
Henri-Marie Dubreuil de Pontbriand	1741-1760

The Fighting Bishop

The Pope, on the recommendation of the Jesuits, named Bishop Laval to lead the church in North America. For the first 15 years he fought openly for church control of the colony, until Louis XIV ended the dispute in 1674 by naming him bishop of New France. This established the church as one of the three powers in the colony, equal to the governor and the intendant. Laval was proud and powerful. For 50 years he squabbled with governors, intendants, councils and parishioners over the power of the Catholic Church in New France. He died at age 85.

Marie among the Hurons

The pioneer nuns were as courageous and devoted as the early priests. The first teaching and nursing nuns were brought to Canada by Madame de La Peltrie and were in the Ursuline order.

Marie de l'Incarnation was one of the first nuns to come to New France. She had been married in France and had had a young son there, but when her husband died, she became a nun and travelled to Canada to help teach the native people about God. In 1640 she wrote:

In France I almost never took the time to read a story and now I must read and think in the language of the Indians. We study this strange language like young children going to school to learn Latin...We are in good health and sing better than they do in France. The air is excellent — this is heaven on earth, even the thorns are full of love.

But life was not always comfortable for the Ursuline nuns. In the summer of 1670 Marie wrote:

All the winters are very cold in this country, but the last one was unusually severe...we have not known a worse winter...there was still ice in the garden in June...God wants us to suffer here and live in sweetness in heaven later. After 32 years in this country we are used to the hard life and have had time to forget the easy life in our old home in France.

Today Canadians can visit the reconstructed settlement of Marie among the Hurons at Penetanguishene, Ontario, and see how the early settlers lived.

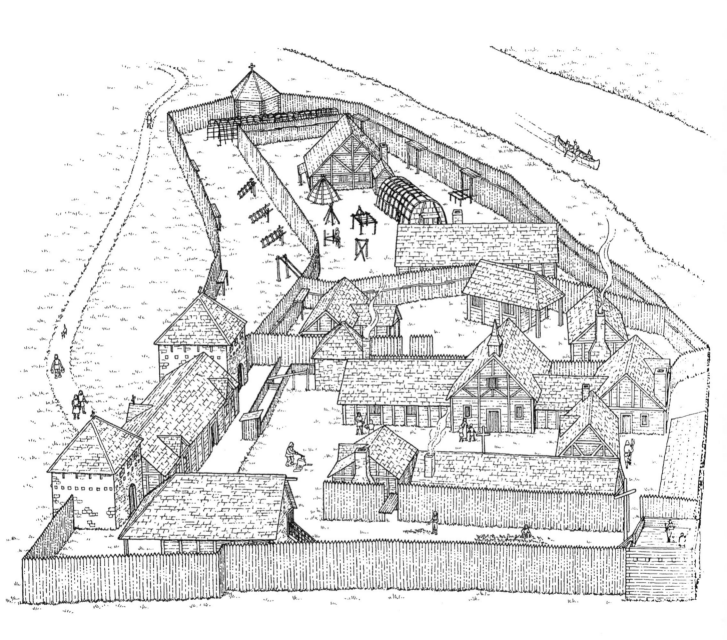

37

Peaceful Natives

Although the stories of Indian torture sound terrible to us today, that was how the Indians proved their bravery, and the tortures were no worse than those used in French or English prisons such as the Bastille or the Tower of London at that time in history. The Iroquois were really a peace-loving people who attacked the French to protect their land. In fact, the Union of the Iroquois Five Nations was called "the great peace" and had been formed by their famous political and religious leader Hiawatha. Its aim was to abolish war completely. Each tribe elected members to a central government, and later the conquered Hurons and Erie Indians were welcomed into the alliance, as well as the Tuscaroras, who were pushed out of North Carolina by the whites.

Bottomless

New France was a unique community that developed its own customs and social behaviour. Here is a humorous example. The bishop of Quebec was forced to issue the following statement to the inhabitants of Ville Marie, who had adopted an unusual habit on hot summer days:

It is with great sorrow that we learned upon
Our return from France of The Bad Habit
you had acquired against all Well-being
of appearing in underwear without bottoms
during the summer to avoid The Great Heat.

Make a Quill Pen

Writing with a Quill Pen

The settlers in New France wrote their letters and journals with pens made from goose quills. You can make and write with your own quill pen.

What you need:

a large wing feather from a goose, turkey or other large bird
pen knife or hobby knife
ink
paper

What to do:

1. Use the knife to trim the end of the quill to the shape shown in Figure 1. Make a small slit in the end of the quill (this helps the ink flow).

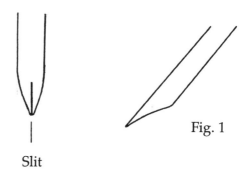

Fig. 1

Slit

2. Dip the end of your pen in the ink and, holding the pen as shown in Figure 2, begin writing. Practise different letters and strokes until you get the feel of using the pen. Your library will have books on calligraphy that will help you.

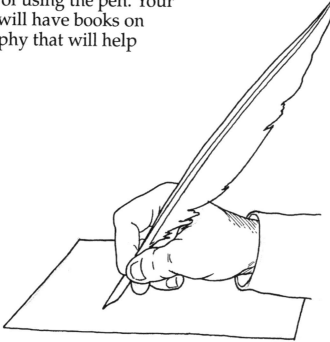

Fig. 2

Writing Jesuit Relations

The records kept by the Jesuits, called *Relations*, are the major reason we have a clear picture of life in New France. The priests kept detailed, hand-written descriptions of personalities and events. Write your own family, school or neighbourhood *Relations*. If you make yourself a quill pen, you can truly feel what it was like to record history in the 1600s. Write once a day.

1. Events: The Jesuit *Relations* recorded events that took place in New France much the way we would write a letter today. Some modern examples:

My sister passed her driver's test today. Now she will be able to drive the family car.
A new family moved into the old Robertson house today.
Mr. McQuade, our social science teacher, was sick today.

2. Personalities: The Jesuit letters described the personalities in the colony. Some modern examples:

Kara was nervous before her driver's test, but now she is acting like a big shot.

Ms. Jennings is not as strict as Mr. McQuade, so we talk more in class, but she doesn't tell funny jokes the way he does. The new kids in the Robertson house seem very shy.

3. Opinions: The Jesuits would often suggest changes or new ideas for the colony. Some modern examples:

I think our family should get a second TV set.
Our school should have more field trips.
The police should give more tickets to drivers who speed up and down our street at night.

CHAPTER 4 *Battle at Long Sault*

Dollard des Ormeaux

When Sieur de Maisonneuve, the governor of Ville Marie (present-day Montreal), heard that Iroquois warriors were gathering on the Ottawa and Richelieu rivers to attack his colony, he summoned Dollard des Ormeaux, his garrison commander, to discuss the defence of the fort.

Much to Maisonneuve's surprise, the young officer had already thought of a plan. He wanted to take a small force up the Ottawa River to attack the Iroquois before they could organize an assault. This would give the colony time to prepare its defences.

With Maisonneuve's approval, Dollard chose 16 unmarried youths, local farmers and artisans, and pushed up the river to meet the gathering enemy. Whispers of his mission floated through the quiet forests ahead of him, and he was soon joined by Chief Anahotaha with 40 Huron braves, and Chief Mitiwemeg with four Algonquins. These men were seeking revenge against the Iroquois, who had killed hundreds of their people.

On May 1, 1660, the small party reached an abandoned stockade at the Long Sault Rapids about 500 km (300 mi.) north of Montreal (just below Hawkesbury, Ontario) and prepared to defend it.

Their first encounter was with an Iroquois scouting party. They killed all but one; the survivor escaped to warn the main war party.

Dollard heard the swish of hundreds of paddles before he caught sight of the Iroquois. Fear gripped him as a force of 300 warriors rounded the bend and came at the fort. The Iroquois suffered heavy losses in the face of French muskets on the first assault, but they attacked two more times before retreating.

There followed five days of silence and confinement, with only the buzzing of flies to break the stillness. Lack of food and water caused most of the Hurons inside the fort to desert, but their chief and a handful of braves remained with the 17 young Frenchmen.

On the fifth day reinforcements of Iroquois, 800 strong, arrived from the Richelieu River. With these new numbers, they launched a full frontal assault, but the valiant group behind the flimsy wooden barricade beat them off.

The Iroquois waited another agonizing three days before the final attack on May 26, 1660. Then they came from all sides, reached the base of the stockade and set fire to the walls. As his men fought hand-to-hand using their muskets as clubs, Dollard prepared a hastily constructed bomb of gunpowder. After lighting it, he tried to throw it over the barricade into the midst of the attackers. It fell short, bounced off the stockade walls and blew up in the faces of the defenders. Several were killed; others were burned or blinded.

Seizing on the moment of confusion, the Iroquois swarmed over the stockade walls, killing all but four Hurons and five Frenchmen, who were later tortured to death.

It was the famous *coureur de bois* Pierre Radisson*, returning from his trip to Hudson Bay, who discovered the gruesome remains at Long Sault. He reported to Maisonneuve that the river was clear of Iroquois; the warriors had given up their plans of attacking Ville Marie after losing one-third of their force against only a handful of young men.

Dollard and his followers had saved the early settlement of Montreal.

* You can read about Pierre Radisson in a previous book in this series, *The Fur Traders*.

Hero or Scoundrel?

There are some historians who say that Dollard was not a hero at all. They claim that he did not go up the river to defend Ville Marie but to steal furs.

Build a Fort

What you need:
scissors
hobby knife
white glue
crayons or felt markers

What to do:

1. Colour the pieces to be cut out. Be careful not to colour the glue tabs. Suggestions: walls of stockade and house — brown. Roofs of towers and house — tan.

2. Cut out the stockade wall pieces. Score them along the top and glue each piece back to back. Do not use too much glue or it will cause the paper to wrinkle.

3. Cut out the pieces for the four towers. Use a hobby knife to cut the slots for the wall tabs. Assemble the towers. (Apply glue only to the tabs, never to the pieces themselves.)

4. Assemble the house.

5. Insert the wall tabs into the four towers and glue them in place.

6. Cut the centre line in the gate so that it can be folded back.

7. Glue your fort to a small piece of cardboard. You may now landscape the fort as you wish.

Wall Assembly

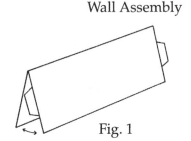

Fig. 1

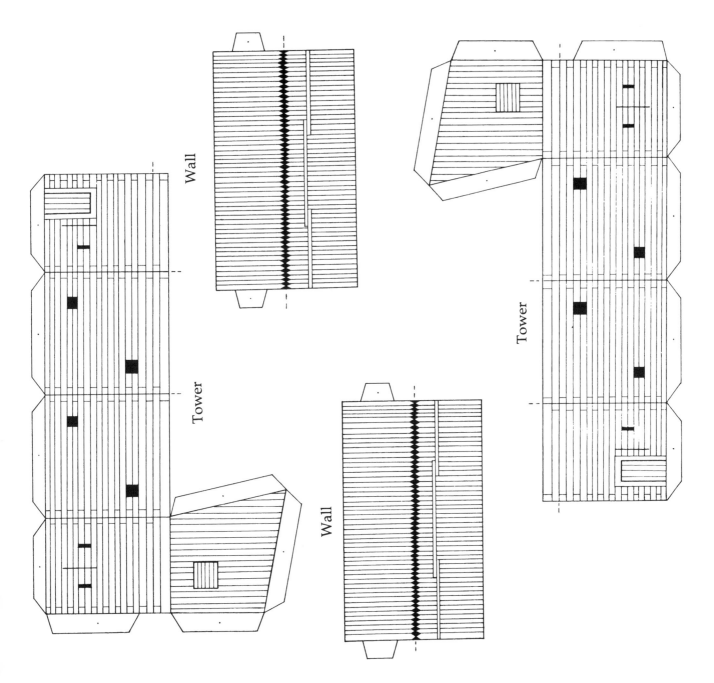

Wall

Tower

Wall

Tower

47

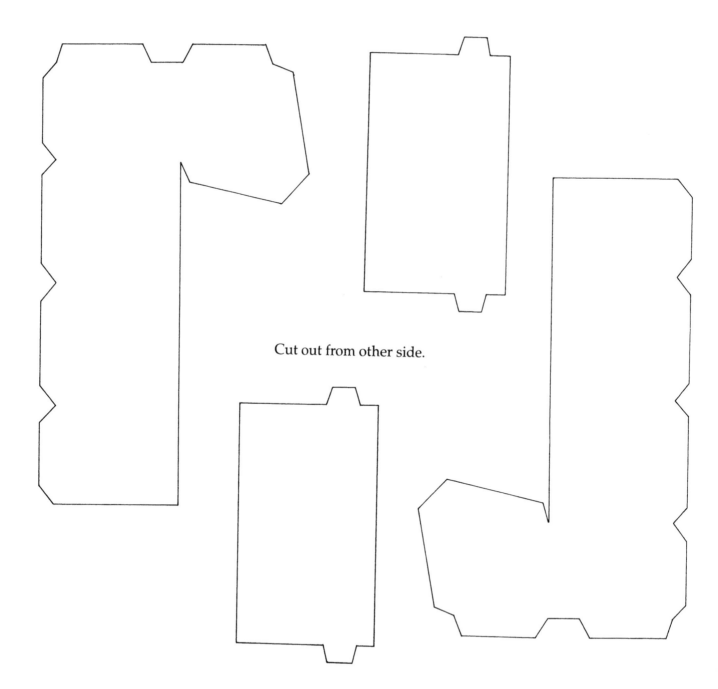

Cut out from other side.

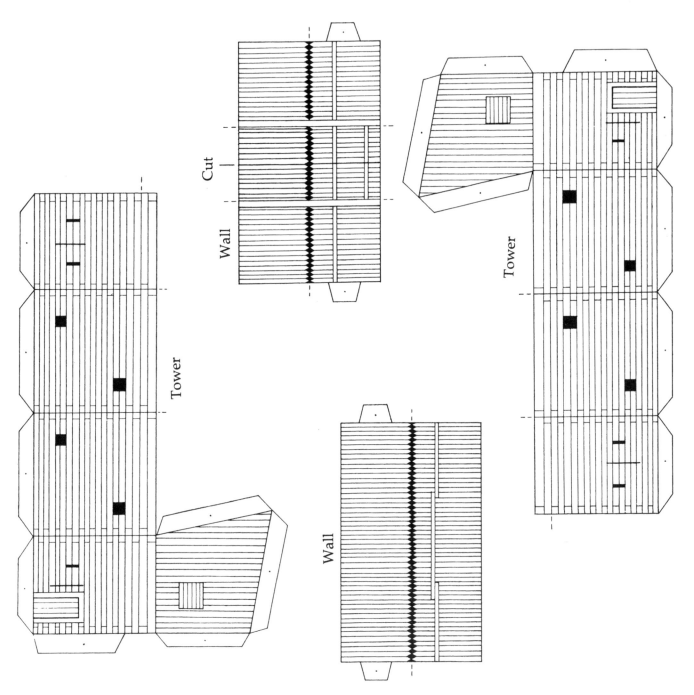

Cut

Wall

Tower

Wall

Tower

49

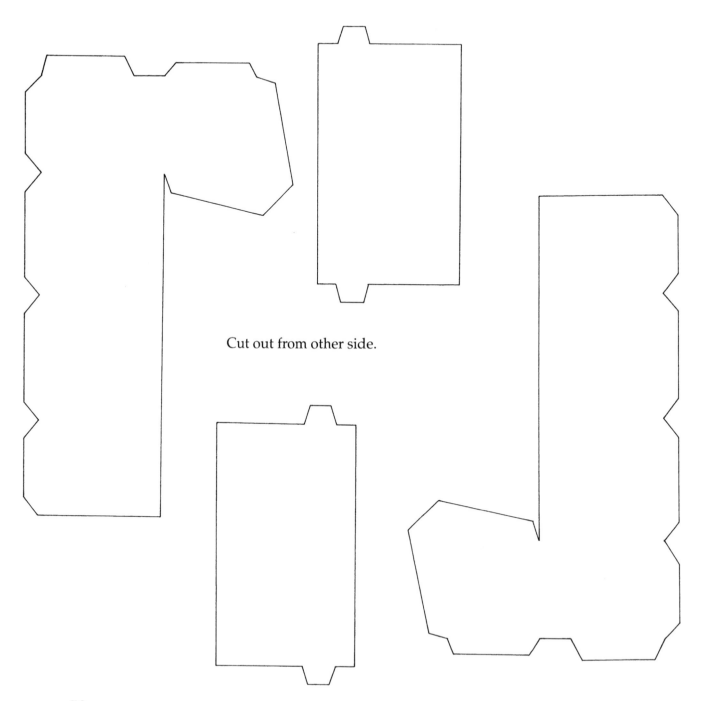

Cut out from other side.

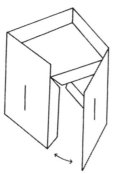

Tower Assembly

Fig. 2

Roof

Chimney

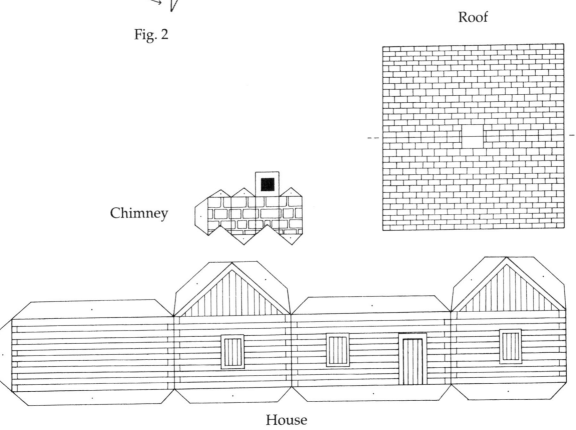

House

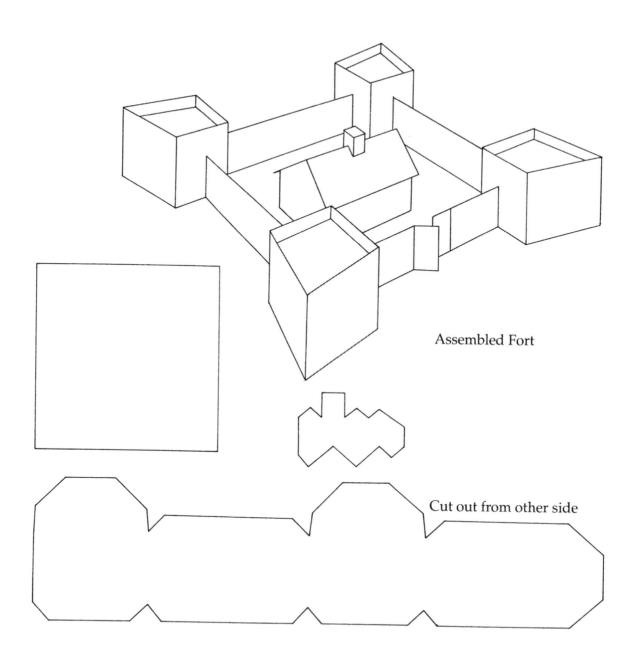

Assembled Fort

Cut out from other side

CHAPTER **5** *The Great Intendant*

Jean Talon

Can you imagine most of the people in North America today speaking French? From 1600 to 1750 it seemed as if that would be the case. What started as small colonies and forts grew and expanded until New France included most of the North American continent.

In 1663 young Louis XIV decided to build a stronger French empire in North America. New France was declared a royal province and the first intendant, Jean Talon, was placed in charge. With the new organization, there were three powerful persons in the province: the bishop, watching over religious and moral education; the governor, providing military protection; and the intendant, ensuring that the colony established a justice system, prospered economically and expanded in population.

The first problem was the Iroquois, who were determined to rid their homeland of the French intruders. The settlers were unable to wander out of sight of their forts or homes for fear of being captured or killed. The Indians regularly raided and burned French houses and crops.

In the summer of 1665 one of France's best army regiments, in grey-and-purple uniforms, paraded down the streets of Quebec, and shiploads of new settlers and supplies arrived with them. The army, commanded by Viceroy de Tracy, later attacked and burned the Indian villages until the native people agreed to a peace treaty.

Once secure, the colony expanded rapidly under Jean Talon. Using the seigneurial system that existed in France, he gave the rich *seigneurs* large tracts of land only if they brought *habitants* to clear them and build homes along the rivers. The *habitants* had to pay rent, a *tithe*, to their *seigneur* and donate a portion, one-twenty-sixth, of their crops to support the local parish (church).

To encourage population growth, Talon offered 20 *livres*, a dowry of money from the king, to any woman who was married before she was 16 and to any man before he was 20. In addition there were financial rewards for families with ten or more children. When a shipload of young women arrived from France, Talon forbade any bachelors to leave the colony to go hunting or to trade furs until the young women were married.

Each *habitant* had to have access to riverwater for his crops and cattle, as well as for transportation. So the *seigneurs* divided their land grants into long narrow strips. Soon the riverbank between Montreal and Quebec was a solid line of whitewashed, steep-roofed *habitant* dwellings.

Not only was the population increasing, but the territory of New France was expanding. In the second book in this series, *The Fur Traders*, you discovered how Pierre Radisson journeyed north to Hudson Bay in 1659 and the La Vérendrye brothers reached the Rocky Mountains of Wyoming in 1743. In 1672 Marquette and Jolliet reached the Mississippi River, and in the next chapter, you will read about La Salle reaching the Gulf of Mexico.

Hudson
Bay

Canada

FRENCH TERRITORY

Quebec
Montreal

Acadia

British Colonies

Louisiana

New Orleans

NEW FRANCE
IN 1712

The King's Daughters

One of Jean Talon's main objectives was to increase the population of New France. Since the major part of the population was unmarried settlers and soldiers, he persuaded the king to import shiploads of *filles du roi* — "king's daughters."

At first these were French orphans from state institutions or women who had no one to support them. Later they included peasant girls and city women who volunteered to voyage to New France in the hope of starting a new life.

The "bride ships" arrived once a year from 1665 to 1671, carrying more than 100 women. Each brought with her a dowry from the king: an ox, a cow, 2 pigs, 2 chickens, 2 barrels of salt beef and 11 crowns in cash.

When they arrived in New France, the women were taken to locations where the young men could meet them and they could ask one another questions to find out if they would make good wives or husbands. Priests and notaries stood by, ready to marry them immediately. If a bachelor proposed marriage, a king's daughter rarely refused. Once married, the young woman became the property of her husband. According to the law in New France, she could never obtain a divorce or separation unless her husband "beat her with a stick thicker than his wrist."

Only 15 of the first 150 women could not find husbands; they became domestic servants. Talon fined women at the age of 16 and men at the age of 20 if they were not married. Couples who had 10 children were rewarded with a pension of 300 *livres* a year; those with 12 received 400 *livres*. Talon reported to the king that within a year most of the brides were pregnant. By 1670 700 babies were born each year.

Talon seized land grants from absentee landlords who had failed to bring out settlers, and divided them into pie-shaped lots that he gave to the young families. The centre of each pie became a small village-fortress so that the settlers could defend themselves against Indian attacks. Each family had to clear one hectare (two acres) for itself and another hectare for a future family.

Talon's plan worked. In 1666, for example, when their military service ended, over 400 soldiers took brides and land grants, rather than return to France.

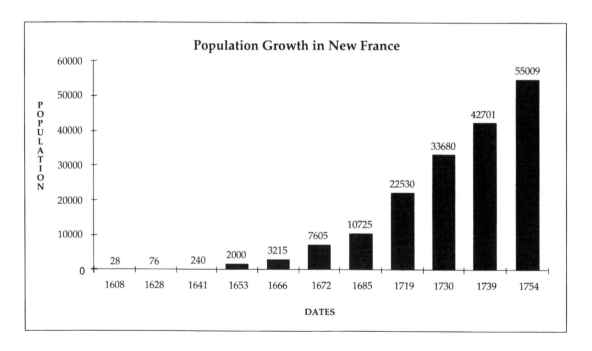

Bachelor of New France

Jean Talon's ideas of "bride ships," fines for unmarried youths and rewards for large families caused the settlement of New France to flourish. However, he himself was a bachelor all his life, until his death at the age of 68.

Card Money

In 1685 Intendant Jacques de Meulles had to pay the soldiers in New France, but the pay-ship had not yet arrived from Europe. He solved the problem by paying the troops with playing cards, which became legal money in the colony for the next twenty-five years.

Multi-cultural Immigrants

Not all the settlers in New France were French. One ship brought a group that included German, Portuguese, Dutch and Algerian immigrants.

Intendants of New France	
Jean Talon	1665-1668
Claude de Bouteroue	1668-1670
Jean Talon	1670-1672
Jacques Duchesneau	1675-1682
Jacques de Meulles	1682-1686
Jean Bochart de Champigny	1686-1702
François de Beauharnois	1702-1705
Jacques and Antoine Raudot	1705-1711
Michel Bégon	1712-1726
Claude Thomas Dupuy	1726-1728
Gilles Hocquart	1731-1748
François Bigot	1748-1760

French Moose

In 1665 Jean Talon brought 14 stallions and mares to New France to help with the farming. Although there were thousands of cattle in the colony at that time, this was the first time the Indians had seen horses; they called them "French moose."

First Events

When a new country is being settled many firsts are recorded in its early history. Here are some firsts in Canada's history:

First Priests – 1615
Four Recollect missionaries arrived at Tadoussac.

First Settler – 1617
Louis Hébert owned a drug-store in Paris but decided to sail to Port Royal with Champlain in the summer of 1606. He spent half his time farming and the other half acting as doctor. In 1613 he moved with his wife and three children to Quebec.

First Marriage – 1617
The first recorded marriage in New France was Stephen Jonquest's to Anne Hébert.

First Church – 1620
The Recollects built the first chapel at Quebec, Notre-Dame-Anges.

First Jesuit *Relation* – 1623
The first stories of life in the colonies were published in France.

First Métis – 1625
Before he met and married Marie, Charles La Tour became the father of the first Métis (half-white, half-native) child in New France. The mother was a Micmac Indian.

First *Seigneurs* – 1634

The first *seigneuries* were in Acadia; Poutrincourt established one in the Annapolis Valley from 1610 to 1614. Robert Giffard was granted Beauport, the first *seigneurie* at Quebec, in 1634.

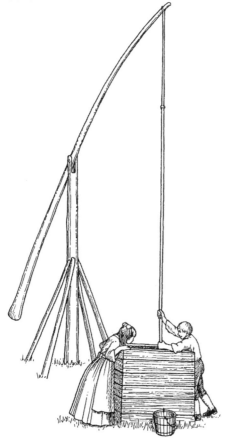

A Sweep Well

First Play – 1640

Martial Piraube was the lead actor in the first play in Quebec. It was written and produced by Marc Lescarbot, who also wrote the first history of New France.

First Birth – 1648

The first white child born in New France was Barbe Meusnier.

First Tavern – 1648

Jacques Brisson opened a licenced tavern in Quebec.

First Execution – 1654

A 16-year-old female thief was the first person to be executed in New France.

First School – 1658

The first public school was opened in a stable in Montreal and run by Marguerite Bourgeoys.

Stone windmills were used as fortresses in times of war or Indian uprisings.

First Ship – 1679
La Salle built the first ship, the *Griffon*, and launched it on the Great Lakes.

First Water Mill – 1691
The first commercial water mill was built at Petit Pré near Quebec.

First Mail – 1721
The first regular mail service was started between Quebec and Montreal.

First Forges – 1737
To refine local iron ore, forges were built at St-Maurice.

First Road – 1737
The rivers had been the only highways in the colony until this road was built between Quebec and Montreal.

Test Your French

The following is a list of jobs in New France in 1663. How many of the jobs can you identify from the French words? The English is on page 89.

1. *Armurier* —
2. *Arpenteur* —
3. *Bedeau* —
4. *Boucher* —
5. *Boulanger* —
6. *Briquetier* —
7. *Chapelier* —
8. *Charbonnier* —
9. *Charpentier* —
10. *Charron* —
11. *Chaudronnier* —
12. *Chirurgien* —
13. *Commis* —
14. *Cordonnier* —
15. *Coutelier* —
16. *Cuisinier* —
17. *Défricheur* —
18. *Domestique* —
19. *Drapier* —
20. *Farinier* —
21. *Fermier* —
22. *Huissier* —

23. *Juge* —
24. *Laboureur* —
25. *Maçon* —

37. *Tisserand* —
38. *Tixier* —
39. *Tonnelier* —
40. *Travailleur* —

26. *Marchand* —
27. *Matelot* —
28. *Menuisier d'art* —
29. *Meunier* —
30. *Mouleur* —
31. *Notaire* —
32. *Prêtre* —
33. *Religieuse* —
34. *Sage-femme* —
35. *Soldat* —
36. *Tailleur d'habits* —

CHAPTER 6 — Searching for China

Sieur de La Salle

Most young people have a goal or dream in their lives, something they would like to do or see or become in the future. The dream of one French youth, René-Robert Cavelier, Sieur de La Salle, was to travel to the mysterious Orient.

René-Robert, the second son of a wholesale merchant, was a good student and his mathematical skills were excellent. At the age of 15, he began studying to become a Jesuit priest. The imaginative and restless boy persistently sent letters to his superiors, asking to be sent to the Jesuit missions in China, but his requests were rejected. Disappointed, the hot-tempered young man left the Jesuits and sailed to New France to make his fortune.

His plan was to become the first to reach China by travelling across the unchartered North American continent. He bought a seigneury at the rapids outside Montreal, built a fort and called it *A la Chine!* — This way to China! Today it is the city of Lachine.

Anxiously La Salle pushed westward and created another seigneury, Cataraqui. There he built Fort Frontenac with solid stone walls (at present-day Kingston, Ontario) and started the first shipyards on the Great Lakes.

He could not sail past Niagara Falls, so he had his men carry supplies up the high cliffs to build the *Griffon*, which sailed lakes Erie,

Huron and Michigan. He reached St. Ignace on August 27, 1679, and sent the *Griffon* back to Niagara loaded with a fortune in furs, while he and 14 men continued westward to the upper Mississippi.

The *Griffon* sank with his furs and La Salle was so arrogant and domineering that the men with him mutinied. But he had the friendship of Governor Frontenac, who let him set up trading posts in the Illinois Valley. From there, he explored down the Mississippi, encountering dozens of new Indian tribes and establishing French forts such as Fort Prud'homme in 1682 at present-day Memphis. Finally he reached the Gulf of Mexico. At the present-day city of Venice, Louisiana, he erected a cross and a post bearing the arms of France.

La Salle had more problems: he almost died of fever; an alligator ate one of his men; Indians, who objected to the white men invading their territory, killed others; and Frontenac was replaced by Governor La Barre, who seized Fort Frontenac to pay off La Salle's debts.

He returned to France, where he persuaded the king to return the fort to him and give him a new land grant that extended from Fort Louis on the Illinois River to New Biscay. With four ships, he set sail for the mouth of the Mississippi to establish a new French colony.

But his snobbish, demanding personality caused him to fight with his sea captain, the Spanish captured one of his ships and he ended up in Texas, unable to locate the Mississippi, which would have linked him to his trading forts in Illinois. Again he fell ill with fever and again hostile Indians killed many of his men. The survivors began to hate and blame him for their failure and misfortune.

Tension and frustration grew as new attempts to locate the Mississippi failed. His haughty and self-centred personality created distrust and contempt. Finally his followers turned against him.

The situation exploded on March 19, 1687, near present-day Nevasoto, Texas. It was a petty argument over freshly killed buffalo meat. La Salle's young nephew, Moranget, who was "more Hot than Wise," took the meat from the hunters, who then murdered him in his sleep. When La Salle came looking for his nephew, the mutineers hid behind bushes. While one of them shouted insults to lure him into the trap, another shot La Salle in the back.

Thus ended the forty-four-year life of La Salle, who never reached China, but who expanded the territory of New France west to the Illinois Valley and south to the Gulf of Mexico.

Conquering North America

The Conquest of North America

This is a game of conquest. The object of the game is to conquer all of North America!

What you need:

2 or 3 players
1 die from a pair of dice
some paper
pencil
scissors

What to do:

1. Make six 2-cm squares from paper and mark them with a symbol for each player. These are your "armies."

2. Draw the board on page 71 on a larger sheet of paper.

How to play:

1. Throw the die to determine which player begins choosing territory. Place an "army" in each territory chosen. Take turns choosing until all the territories are occupied.

2. Throw the die again to determine who begins the attack.

3. The attacker announces which enemy territory they wish to attack and *from* which one of their territories. Each player then throws the die. If the attacker wins, the defender's army is removed and replaced with one of his or hers. If the defender wins, the army from the territory from which the attack began is removed and replaced with one of the defender's armies.

4. The die passes to the next player, who begins his or her attack. The game continues until one player controls the entire continent.

* For a longer game you may divide North America into 12 parts and give each player 12 armies.

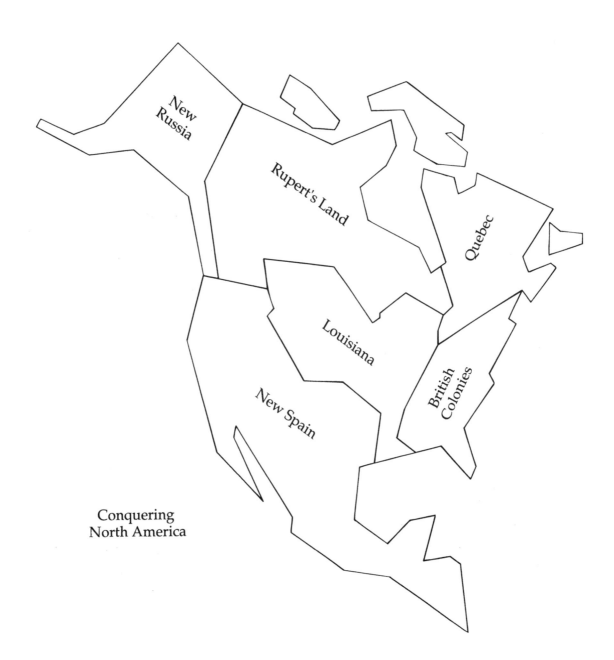

New
Russia

Rupert's Land

Quebec

Louisiana

British
Colonies

New Spain

Conquering
North America

7 *A Young Heroine*

Madeleine de Verchères

It is not unusual today for a young teenager to be left in charge of the family home or younger brothers or sisters for a short time, but in New France teenagers were considered adults and expected to take their share of adult responsibility.

From 1689 to 1701 the Iroquois once again declared war on the French settlements and Governor Frontenac returned to defend the colony.

On October 22, 1692, 14-year-old Madeleine de Verchères was working in the field with the other men and women along the St. Lawrence River, 32 km (20 mi.) below Montreal. On the other side of the field, the seigneurial fort of the Verchères protectively overshadowed the scene. François Jarret de Verchères was on military duty in Quebec and his wife, Marie, was visiting in Montreal.

There was no warning. The Indians sprang from the forest with loud war whoops, their tomahawks raised. Madeleine ran with the speed and instinct of a frightened fawn toward the fortress in which she had been born. The dying screams of her fellow workers were lost in the sound of the wind whistling past her ears. Her heart was pounding hard as she reached the entrance of the fort.

Her screams of "To arms! To arms!" were suddenly silenced by a heavy tug on her shawl that jerked her to a halt. One Iroquois, swifter than the others, had caught up with her and now held the

73

other end of her streaming shawl in his grasp. Madeleine desperately tore herself loose from the garment and bolted inside the barricade, slamming the gate in the face of her pursuer. No one else had escaped with her.

Forty or 50 Iroquois warriors were outside the fort; there were only two soldiers and some women and children inside. The two men were preparing to blow up themselves and the others, rather than risk being captured and tortured.

Disgusted and furious, Madeleine scolded them about their lack of courage. Two years earlier she had watched her mother defend the fort against an Indian raid that had lasted a couple of days. Now Madeleine prepared for a siege. She ordered the two soldiers to take positions on the walls and armed the women along with an 80-year-old servant and her two younger brothers, aged 10 and 12.

Unexpectedly a cry came from one of the defenders. A small boat had landed at the dock below the fort. Madeleine recognized the visitors, who were unaware of the danger. She rushed from the fort, met them on the jetty and hurried them to safety. The Indians, taken by surprise at her sudden action, failed to act.

For eight days and nights the small group held off the enemy, until, on the ninth day, Captain La Monerie arrived from Montreal with a force of 40 men to chase away the attackers. The captain was greatly impressed. He reported that the defences of the fort were as well organized as if a king's officer had been in command.

News of young Madeleine's heroic actions spread throughout New France and she was awarded a Royal Pension by Governor Frontenac.

Long before the final battle on the Plains of Abraham, the English and French had competed fiercely over the new continent. Usually the wars originated in Europe and spread to the colonies, and frequently, captured territories in North America were returned in European peace treaties.

In 1613 Samuel Argall was sent to push the French out of Acadia and destroyed Port Royal.

In 1628 a British fleet led by a Scotsman, David Kirke, captured Quebec and took Champlain prisoner; however, the English gave Quebec back to the French in 1633 and Champlain returned to govern.

In 1654 an English force captured Fort La Tour and Acadia.

In 1662 the French started a colony in Newfoundland at Placentia Bay.

In 1670 Prince Rupert of England claimed all the lands around Hudson Bay and James Bay.

In **1672** La Salle established Fort Frontenac at present-day Kingston, Ontario.

In **1683** Pierre Radisson led a French attack and captured the Hudson's Bay Company's Fort Nelson.

In **1684** Radisson's partner, Groseilliers, surrendered Fort Bourbon (Fort York) to the English.

In **1686** d'Iberville seized Hudson's Bay Company forts.

In **1687** Denonville attacked the Senecas, who were allies of the English, and built Fort Niagara.

In **1690** Frontenac attacked and destroyed English settlements. In the same year the Massachusetts militia, led by William Phips, captured Port Royal from the French. However, when the English tried to take Quebec, Frontenac defeated them.

In **1694** d'Iberville led a French attack that recaptured Fort Bourbon.

In **1700** Cadillac built Fort Pontchartrain at present-day Detroit.

In **1704** a French force led by de Rouville attacked and burned the English settlement at Deerfield, Massachusetts.

In **1708** the French captured St. John's in Newfoundland.

In 1710 the English captured Port Royal and renamed it Annapolis Royal.

In 1713 the Treaty of Utrecht gave all the territories of Nova Scotia, Newfoundland and the Hudson Bay to England.

In 1717 the French founded a fortress at Louisbourg on Cape Breton Island.

In 1738 the French built Fort Rouge (Winnipeg) and Fort La Reine (Portage-La-Prairie) in present-day Manitoba.

In 1744 French forces from Louisbourg attacked Annapolis Royal.

In 1745 an English army captured Louisbourg, but the Treaty of Aix-la-Chapelle returned it to the French in 1748.

In 1749 Cornwallis created an English naval base at Halifax.

In 1752 the French built Fort Rouillé at present-day Toronto.

In 1754 the English troops led by George Washington were defeated when they attacked Fort Duquesne.

In 1755 the French Acadians were expelled from Nova Scotia.

In 1756 Montcalm arrived in Canada and captured Fort Oswego.

In 1757 Montcalm won another victory at Fort William Henry on Lake George.

In 1758 Montcalm with only 3,000 men defended Fort Ticonderoga against a British force of 16,000.

In 1758 the British captured Louisbourg.

In1758 Fort Frontenac was captured by the English.

In 1759, the same year as the Battle of the Plains of Abraham, the British captured Fort Niagara and the French deserted Fort Rouillé.

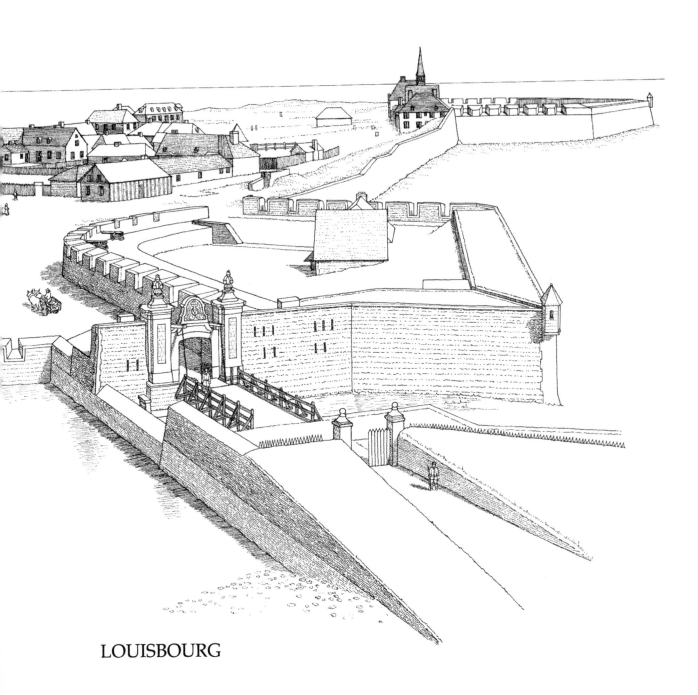

LOUISBOURG

Expulsion of the Acadians

When war began in 1755, the British were in control of Acadia (Nova Scotia and New Brunswick), but the people were mainly French and hostile. When the French settlers refused to sign an oath of allegiance to the British, their farms were burned and they were forced to leave the colony under armed guard. The French settlers saw what was happening, changed their minds and offered to sign the oath. But they were told it was too late. They were dispersed among the English colonies along the Atlantic seaboard from Labrador to Florida.

Soldier of France

Pierre Le Moyne d'Iberville has been called the "most famous guerrilla leader of his time." In 1682, when he was only 21, he was leading attacks against the English forts on Hudson Bay. For 15 years he plagued the English fur traders in the northwest, winning victories at sea as well as on land. Then he turned his forces against Newfoundland, destroying 36 of the 38 English settlements. The military might of d'Iberville ensured France's claim to the Louisiana Territory and defeated the British in the Caribbean. He died in Cuba at age 45 of an unknown disease.

New France Crossword Puzzle

ACROSS:

2. An Italian sea captain who claimed Newfoundland for the English in 1497
7. The name of the home that Champlain built at Quebec
8. The name of the original Indian village at Quebec
9. The name of the original Indian village at Montreal
11. The first intendant
14. A rich landowner
16. The leader who died at Long Sault
17. A farmer who owned his own land in New France
21. The English general who defeated Montcalm
22. The governor of New France who was a friend to La Salle

DOWN:

1. An Indian chief who was kidnapped by Cartier
2. The French sea captain who arrived first in New France
3. The man who followed a river to the Gulf of Mexico
4. The original meaning of the word "Canada"
5. A nun who taught the Huron Indians
6. The French fortress on Cape Breton Island
10. A 13-year-old girl who defended a fort against an Indian attack
12. The name of the husband and wife who fought to control Acadia
13. An instrument used by early explorers to calculate their positions
15. The first ship built on the Great Lakes
17. A "French moose"
18. The patron saint of Canada
19. French people who were forced to leave their homes in Nova Scotia
20. The first *coureur de bois*

CHAPTER 8 *The Plains of Abraham*

Wolfe and Montcalm

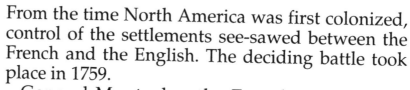

From the time North America was first colonized, control of the settlements see-sawed between the French and the English. The deciding battle took place in 1759.

General Montcalm, the French commander, waited behind the walls of his fortress at Quebec as the English fleet, led by General Wolfe, anchored off the Island of Orléans in the St. Lawrence River. Both generals were experienced soldiers who had proven their military abilities.

The task confronting Wolfe seemed impossible. The Quebec stronghold was protected by natural barriers of rivers and cliffs, and was defended by an army of 16,000 men. Wolfe, with only 9,000 soldiers, made a frontal invasion on the city but was forced back.

Wolfe waited three months before making a second major attack. In the dark hours before dawn on September 13, 1759, he daringly led an army of 5,000 ashore at the base of the high cliffs at a place known today as Wolfe's Cove. They climbed the treacherous cliffs that led to the French fortress high above. By morning they were lined up on the Plains of Abraham facing the walled city of Quebec.

The French, weakened by three months of siege, were taken by surprise. Montcalm decided to attack immediately, hoping to push the English back over the cliffs to the river below.

THE PLAINS OF ABRAHAM
QUEBEC
September 13, 1759

Wolfe calmly waited until the French were only 12 m (40 ft.) away before he gave the order for his first line to fire. Struck in the wrist by a bullet, he paused only to wrap his wound in a handkerchief. After 20 minutes, the French retreated. Leading the right line in pursuit, Wolfe was hit in the chest by two bullets and died almost immediately. His army went on to capture Quebec.

Montcalm, protecting the rear of his escaping troops, was also shot during the battle. Nevertheless he mounted his jet-black horse and was helped back to safety by his men. As he lay dying, aware of his defeat, Montcalm sent a message to the English asking them to be kind to the wounded French. He was dead by the next morning, and New France came under British rule.

The Final Battle

With the death of Montcalm and the capture of Quebec, the French forces in New France were under the command of Gaston de Lévis, who won a victory at Ste-Foy in April 1760 and forced the British to retreat behind the walls of Quebec. Now their positions were reversed. It was the French army laying siege outside and the English defending the fortress at Quebec. Both France and England sent a fleet of ships to support their soldiers. By mid-May all British and French eyes were anxiously focused on the St. Lawrence River. Whichever fleet got there first would decide the victory. It was the British fleet that arrived after capturing and burning six French ships in the Gulf of St. Lawrence.

Answers to New France Crossword Puzzle, page 83

ACROSS

2. Cabot
7. *habitation*
8. Stadacona
9. Hochelaga
11. Talon
14. *seigneur*
16. Dollard
17. *habitant*
21. Wolfe
22. Frontenac

DOWN

1. Donnacona
2. Cartier
3. La Salle
4. village
5. Marie
6. Louisbourg
10. Madeleine
12. La Tour
13. astrolabe
15. *Griffon*
17. horse
18. Brébeuf
19. Acadians
20. Brûlé

English words for the jobs in New France on pages 64 and 65.

1. gun maker
2. land surveyor
3. church warden
4. butcher
5. baker
6. brick maker
7. hat maker
8. coal seller
9. carpenter
10. wheel maker
11. coppersmith
12. doctor (surgeon)
13. shop clerk
14. shoemaker
15. knife maker
16. cook (chef)
17. land clearer
18. female servant
19. cloth seller
20. flour seller
21. farmer
22. public official
23. judge
24. farm worker
25. stonecutter
26. merchant
27. sailor
28. cabinet maker
29. miller
30. blacksmith
31. lawyer
32. priest
33. nun
34. midwife
35. soldier
36. tailor
37. weaver of cloth
38. spinner of wool
39. barrel maker
40. labourer

Index